Under the Influence of Water

Wayne State University Press, Detroit

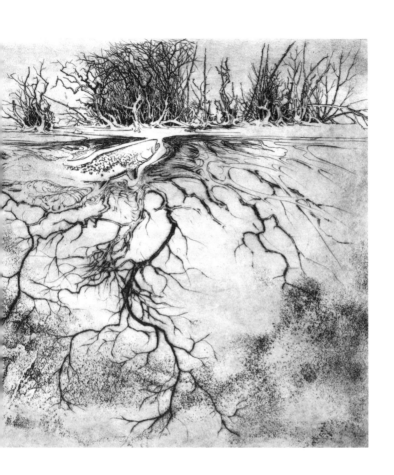

Under the Influence of Water

Poems, Essays, and Stories

Michael Delp

Illustrations by Ladislav R. Hanka

GREAT LAKES BOOKS

A complete listing of the books in this series can be found at the back of this volume.

Philip P. Mason, Editor
Walter P. Reuther Library, Wayne State University

Dr. Charles K. Hyde, Associate Editor
Department of History, Wayne State University

03   02   01   4   3   2

Library of Congress Cataloging-in-Publication Data

Delp, Michael.
    Under the influence of water : poems, essays, and stories
/Michael Delp.
      p. cm. – (Great Lakes books)
    ISBN 0-8143-2391-X (pbk. : alk. paper)
    1. Fishing–Great Lakes–Literary collections I. Title.
II. Series.
PS3554.E44447U5 1992
811'.54--dc20   92-10989

Designer: Mary Primeau

Cover art: Ladislav R. Hanka

Many of the poems, stories and essays in this volume appeared in *Traverse the Magazine, Poetry Northwest, Poetry Now, Detroit Magazine, The Flyfisher, Passages North, Riverwatch, Michigan Sports Gazette, The Third Coast: Contemporary Michigan Poetry.*

for my father who taught me how to fish
and for my mother who waited for us every time
and for Claudia and Jaime who wait for me now

Contents

Poems

Essays

Stories

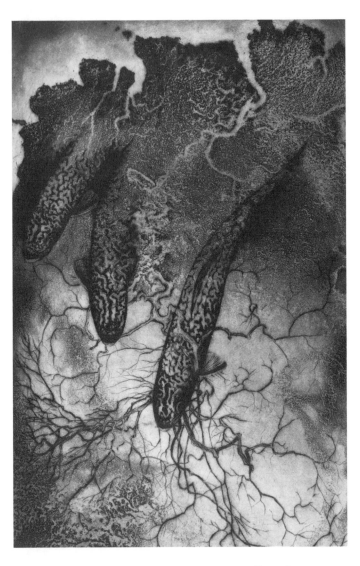

One day, standing in a river with my flyrod,
I'll have the courage to admit my life.

Jim Harrison

Going North

Going north means going
into something deeper than silence.
Mist hangs for hours in the woods
and the apparitions singing in dreams
know places we will never see.
You will know you are north
by the edges of the day
and the slight aura surrounding the trees.
Something in your muscles will be trying
to remember ancient directions,
the way into old hunting grounds,
and if you died
and someone threw your bones
into the water,
they would swim together
and form a long arrow
pointing north.

River: Finding the Way North

1

Even in the rain when the surface pales and becomes covered with wind ripples, you will never know this river. If you floated all the way down it, working your way in and out of the deadfall, you would not come to knowledge. A man standing next to any section of this river will swear he feels a vibration, senses some wild electricity working through his body. There are nights in mid-December when the moonlight glinting off the surface makes it look as though it is covered with fireflies. At times, in August, you can watch the river from a high bank and think it is bottomless. The clarity of the water pulls at you. You bend close to see your reflection and, instead, see further than you have ever seen before.

3 The Leaving

The man and his wife stand on the riverbank. It is early May. The sun is shining. This time, she is leaving for good. They speak, and a distance grows out of their words. The man shuffles his feet and watches the river. Shadows move across the water. Between the man and the woman the day unwinds. The river moves past them. When the car arrives they both walk to the house. There are few words. Finally the woman stiffens her face, dips toward him, and leaves. The man follows her to the car. After she leaves he does not go back inside. He returns to the river, sits down, and watches the water. Something inside him unwinds, trails for miles, and finally snaps. For weeks he will rise early, watch the river, and think that he hears her somewhere in the room. When summer comes he will spend long hours close to the river. He will feel his senses coming back. He will feel them flow and fill places he had forgotten. During the winter he will fall away from his friends. He will grow down into himself. He will learn that when everything else fails, he will still be able to sit and watch the movement of the water. He will learn to trust the river for its constancy. For the rest of his life he will be able to close his eyes and see the river. And late at night, when his sleep is empty and troubled, he will lie back, hear the sounds of water come from far back in his head, and feel his body settle into sleep.

16

4 Fog

You will come to what you swear must be the last
bend in the river. There will be smells in your nostrils
which go beyond description, mixtures of cedar and
mud, and a deep musty odor you will mistake for
the breath of a beautiful woman. This is fog you can
dip your hand into, squeeze together, and come out
with nothing. How strange, you think, not to see your
hand at the end of your arm. You conjure up images of
yourself going in, parting the fog just enough to slip
through, finding that spot on the bank where you are
sure she must be sitting. She is cupping her breasts in
her hands as though once there you could replace the
emptiness in your own hands with the soft directions
you are positive must be printed on her chest.

5 Power

This river could kill you, but it won't. It will confuse you. When you think you are riding the flow east, you will really be going west. When you try to take a compass reading, you will be wrong. The river has changed directions so many times in the last hundred years that the sun becomes a mirage. The man who has lived or camped on its banks will tell you that sometimes, late at night, you will have a sudden urge, even in the coldest months of the year, to run to the river for a drink or to lie down on its bottom and make love. There is a power which makes you want to dive to the gut of the river, curl your fingers into the gravel, take a deep breath, and give yourself over.

6 Warning

If all sense of the river erodes away inside you, there will still be the overpowering sense of water. There will be many days when nothing will satisfy your thirst except river water. When you dip a cup and bring it to your mouth, you will come as close as you ever have to purity. When you drink, you feel the water move all the way through you. You will fall silent. Your eyes will stay on the river. Something inside you will drift into an invisible center and that sound you hear will be the sound of your own blood pulsing close to the river.

7 Second Warning

Leave the river. It will stay with you. Miles from its source you will notice the smell of cedar coming from under your skin. The river is like a medicine. The idea of the river packs in close to your life and stays with you as a form of protection. You will always be aware of its presence. In conversations you will suddenly feel your concentration break loose and gather around a particular bend in the river. The river has its own weather, its own sounds, its own way of working into the wells of your memory. The river is always open. It has no reasons. It moves in a shallow bed in the earth, moving like a woman who is always leaving one lover and going to another.

8 Mist

It is too easy to call the river mist an apparition. You can become lost easily in this weather. All your senses will be distorted. You will think you have walked too far, missed a crucial landmark. Your voice will leave your body and make a path through the fog. If you lie down in the river and let your body float downstream you will have a chance to get out. Birds of prey will appear overhead as fast moving, dark shadows. You will become so cold you will want to feel the pain of a talon in your neck. If you can still breathe, take in as much air as possible and let the mist become part of you.

9 Last Warning

This river will tumble through you. It will fill your
eyes and stretch itself into beautiful passages inside
your body. Everything will look clearer. Once the river
enters you, there will be something inside your body
which will never sleep. If you touch the river it will
go around your hand, around your body if you let it.
The man who has been close to the river in all seasons
carries a special knowledge with him. He knows death
is in the water, that it moves along beside the river
like a shadow. This death is like a bridge from the
river to that other place: the darker, tangled regions
of the back country.

10 Back Country

Everything here is river. There are no banks or trees, only endless water flowing north. You will hear birds, but never see them. Fish will leave a flash of riled sand on the bottom. The weather here is a combination of all weather. The wind blows steadily and there is a slight October sharpness to the air. There is only one direction: north. This is where true north begins, where water acquires the taste of iron. There are no trees or swamps. Only water. Even if the earth fell apart, this place would still exist. There are no trails in, no marked waterways. There are no maps. Only stories.

11 Directions

I used to think in terms of pure direction, waiting for my skull bones to find the perfect alignment, the wind hooking around my neck, pulling me into the roots of my senses. Now, I want to sit down by the edge of the river and imagine I have lived in water since birth. I want to wake in the morning and feel water seeping out of my eyes, feel my heart dance and surge with every full moon. I want to say I know this river, safe in the knowledge that even in darkness I might use my mind as a kind of compass, the bones gone resonant, leading me through miles of wilderness.

12 A Story for Someone's Death

It goes this way: for weeks the old man lay in fever. His lips moved continuously, a voice coming from deep in his belly asking for water. If he had been near the river they should have carried him down so he could stretch his old arms full length in the icy water. The deep cracks of his skin would fill with the ointment of pure coldness, and later that night, troubled in a dream of the fire under his skin, he would wake to the taste of the river, the memory of the cold, the way his lips drank it in, the taste of iron turning to blood. He would hear his voice as he had known it before: rich and flowing, the sound of black ice mixing with the howl of the wind, his body cupping into itself, then driven upward, a spike of pure direction churning into white light, his body free and clean.

Casting toward the Light

1

We go in through a half-mile of swamp,
then wait at the salmon pool.
In the half-darkness we begin casting.
We cast perhaps fifty times,
letting the lines drift deep,
our flies rolling along the sandy bottom.

We cast like this for hours.
We cast in the hopes of catching fish.
We cast, perhaps, to throw something
out of ourselves,
believing there is some way to transfer
what we wish we could become
into the way the way we work the river.

2

All day I remember the way the river looked,
how our lines arced through early mist and sunlight.
I think of my phantom self standing hip deep
in the river, trying for that perfect cast,
that one touch of the line that would reach all the way
into this life,
pull me free,
and how maybe every move from now on
should have something to do with ritual of casting,
casting toward the one true part of yourself that
never backed down, or gave in,
the part of yourself that sits somewhere,
maybe deep in a swamp,
waiting for you to slip into a new skin,
as one might move into a large net,

Rainfishing

Everything is gray. He pushes his arm out into a gray kind of air. The fly line, bright yellow, tapers off into a blur, into the gray mist. He begins to think he is fishing inside a dream, perhaps inside the belly of a huge, gray animal. The air smells of dead cedar, swamp, mixed with the smell of gray clay on the banks. His eyes trace the line down the guides, then three feet past the rod tip he is fishing in something entirely unknown. After fifteen or twenty minutes he starts to think something is tricking him. He isn't fishing, but notices the rod has turned to some kind of gray yarn unraveling out of his gray body. Just before nightfall he feels the last bit of himself stretching out, drifting downstream. He thinks of someone finding him as a pile of gray yarn downstream, imagines that he is taken home, put into his wife's hands, forming his face again, putting the gray back into his eyes, knitting a new life.

Hunting the Lake Shore, Bass Lake, 1954

I had a Daisy Scout,
brown plastic stock
and a secret compartment for
BBs.
In the early morning I'd walk the lake,
wait for the bullfrogs to wake up then
plug them clean.

At night, my mother would
strip their skins,
roll each leg in flour and pepper
and we'd stand around the stove,
watch them dance in the skillet,
the room hazing over with the smell
of crisp frog legs.

On the cool nights
we'd light the kerosene stove,
watch the flames hop behind the isinglass,
the shadows jumping up against our legs,
then the frogs would start up,
the voices of bullfrogs calling
up and down the lake,
and my father would go to the porch,
and answer
his voice deep and solid
pumping for all he was worth,
then come in to the stove,
the shadow of his body
leaping back toward the water.

Skinning the Bullheads

It was Charlie Smallenberger who caught them best,
out late at night in the middle of Bass Lake
using tiny silver hooks and balls of rotted hamburger.
He always said you could feel their mouths
turn into perfect circles around the bait,
then he'd reel slow and long,
bringing the bullheads up over the side of the boat.
In the morning we'd watch him at the skinning table,
how he'd nail their tails down and pull their skins
off with a pair of Craftsman pliers,
then come down quick with his hunting knife
for their whiskered heads.
He'd shake their skins at us
and from two feet away
you could see out through their eye holes,
and he'd have maybe twenty of them
white and skinned in the pail
by the time he was done,
the skins slumped in a pile on the ground.

All day you could hear the wild cats from the woods
come into the dump behind his outhouse
how they screeched and snarled,
fought for the biggest skins, the sweet heads.
They carried the skeletons back into the woods,
and when we found a place
where a cat had finished one off,
we always looked for the bones, even a piece,
part of a spine or skull we thought
would give us some kind of power,
some way to keep us safe,
keep our skins on our own backs.

Under the Influence of Water

Lost again, this time
wading through snow on the Pere Marquette,
and up ahead the snow forms into the torso
   of someone
you never had a chance to know.
This is the place they'll find you in the spring:
two legs dancing in the current,
your neck tied with twenty-pound monofilament,
one eye slightly askew, the grin on your face
from a week of torment,
the way you imagined her to come down to you,
how she moved with the movement of the river,
and because she was made of snow:
how her skin settled into your own.

You wash up in your sleep,
your belly white,
eyes opaque like tiny moons
floating in your skull.
You love this ritual,
this way all the women in your life
come to you with intentions of rescue,
how they slip their hands under your head,
letting the river pass over you,
and someone whispers that all the rivers on earth
were once rivers of blood,
and to live once meant finding that one true river,
cutting yourself open,
wading in,
letting the river pass through.

I see them sometimes,
walking the banks when I fish,

their arms raised in a half wave,
their faces contorted.
Even from the middle of the river
I know on each face I see a little of my own,
knowing that these ghosts are only husks,
collections of bad dreams,
lost plans,
remembrances of all the things I never was,
some are the spirits of relatives
dead thirty years too soon,
the ghosts of alcoholics, horse thieves,
prisoners of war.

For hours I have fished and seen them drift
up off bottom,
their huge eyes blue and clear,
then my life feels as if it separates,
half of me goes downstream fishing between dead-
    fallen cedar,
the other half slips in, lies down in familiar arms,
goes back wild to the river.

32 Once, on the Platte,
the moon, stars,
reflected in a cup of whiskey,
the mirror image of one eye looking
through itself,
like peering in the front of a pinhole camera
only you look back,
see your father casting before you were born,
the line moves away from him like light,
and you feel that pull,
how he baptized you with a handful of river water

when you were eight years old,
gave the first drink, then drank himself,
and each movement now is a memory of
how the river moved in you that night,
how your father has river in him,
how your river is the same as your father's.

Maps turn red,
rivers turn into blood,
a body suddenly stands,
is part map:
the ghosts of rivers
haunt the veins,
casting under half moons,
knowing there are fish
struggling out of the heart.

One river seems to fall out of the moon,
the other begins in a photograph from the twenties:
Hemingway in Michigan, stepping off a boxcar,
the flyrod strapped like an antenna to his pack,
headed north, tramping the streams,
each twist of his wrist, each cast arcing toward
that last day in Idaho when the shotgun
lay in his hands, the barrel icy,
a thousand rivers releasing all at once.

33

"Water will never leave earth" you wrote,
and tonight I send what little is left of my spirit
toward that black feeder creek near the house
then sit down inside and watch,
waiting for its return,

thinking how my spirit will look when it comes in the
  back door,
holding a woman made entirely of water,
thinking how my spirit would enter this woman,
run the darker regions inside her,
ride the current of her wildness home.

34

Ice

The first night after your daughter is born,
you dream she has turned to ice,
that there is ice under the bed,
ice in your veins, a heart of ice,
a cold you will carry
locked inside each brain cell.
You dream how you will move for the next sixty years
to the sound of her body melting.

A cold day in late March:
millions of pounds of lake ice
floating on black water, so you go out
lie down and make angels
in the snow, and later, back at the house
you drink through a night storm,
sure you hear the sound of your own wings
moving against the ice,
as if your body were still out there,
flapping on the surface not sure of the way out,
the way in.

I watch the journey with Cousteau
inside the iceberg, begin to believe
they are drifting through a huge heart,
the veins blue and tight,
and think of holding my own frozen heart
in my hands, enough ice there to
cool several drinks, three women,
a small pond,
the forehead of a feverish daughter.

35

Calling the Salmon

The Dream

I slide up from the bottom
of this dream,
reach my hands into the cold air
of the room,
the sound of the river packed like ice
into my ears.
My eyes bend toward the moonlight,
and each thought compresses
around the dream
of swimming inland,
my arms pulling my body
through a dark tunnel of water,
and how the brain dances
with the chemical of this place,
each mark on the river bottom
part of the map,
listening underwater
to the river calling the way,
then sliding out of bed to the pull in my jaw,
the explosion of muscle in my legs
which drives all of me out of the house
toward the sound of moving water.

2 The Bed

I leap toward her,
each movement of my hands
runs close to her skin,
the way she moves over me,
her voice swirling into my ears,
kneeling over my body
as if she could reach down,
pull me from the river under the bed,
feel in her hands
I had come from a long way,
and only later,
when she held me to the light,
would she know the sound coming
out of my throat was a song,
a tale of the way back,
my body lying close to hers,
the man part of me dreaming
of a huge fish waiting,
holding only an instant at the river mouth,
then that first surge,
the heading in,
following a pulse in the darkness.

3 The Song

For years you feel your life
drain down to nothing.
You begin to stare into storms,
try to dig for roots
in the middle of December,
bring the firewood to your lips
and hope there is enough sap left
to get you into the next spring.
It is not a question of growing skins
against the weather,
or stumbling out of your house
at the end of February,
thinking you could lie down under the lake,
find a woman made entirely of ice,
nor is it a question
of knowing less and less each day,
how your mind wants to get
out of its space,
split those old joints in the skull,
just enough to let in a little more light,
and the real question turns
in your head, stays there,
38   its breath cold and dry, lingering,
asking which way out,
which way in?

4 Light

On a Sunday in October you float
the Crystal River,
think you see yourself dead and rotted
at the bottom of each pool.
You believe that if you cut the eye of a salmon
open, you will find a plan,
and so you open your mouth
into the bright sunlight,
bend close to the water
and push out a slow, deep sound.
For a moment you think they have not heard,
then see a swirl of tail far down river,
a huge fin moving upstream
toward your outstretched arms.

In the instant you touch the old scales
on his back you sense that finally,
you know something worth knowing,
know something worth taking back,
and on the drive south along Lake Michigan
you smell the tip of your finger,
notice the tiny slivers of light
caught in your skin.

The Language of Water

Someone said,
if you're born here,
the lakes are in your blood,
and each day of the year
I ask myself if this language I know
comes from a memory of water
and how, in the words I say,
I listen for the slight vibration
of water moving through rock,
rivers breaking up under the earth,
the almost inaudible sound
of water moving under ice,
or the sound a man and a woman make
when they slide together
drifting toward bottom.

Lakes

The summer I was twelve
I swam between Polly Lewis's Legs,
hovered there
as long as I could hold my breath,
watching the way they
slid out of her body,
how the tiny hairs on her thighs
shifted back and forth in the current,
and later, in the cottage,
I peeked through the cracks
in the knotty pine,
watched her dry off,
then fell asleep listening
to the sound of each drop of water
sliding off her suit,
and thought I knew then
if I moved into her,
she would smell of the lake,
each ripple of her skin
rolling like a wave
over my lips.

River Access

Driving the back roads
looking for river access,
the full moon just rising
like a white eye over the horizon,
you want to find some way into the water,
some way to replenish the husk of yourself.

At the wheel you feel like a skeleton,
something rattling with the juice sucked out,
while up ahead in the headlights
you think you see a man made entirely of light
dancing back and forth across the road.

When you squint you see it's really your self,
the eyes sparking,
skin lit up as if you were doing some kind of star
    dance.
When you scream out the window your own name
    rips out
of your mouth, trails for miles behind the car.

You want to get out,
howl a little,
lie down in the bath of moonlight
and wash the man out of you,
rub yourself with coyote scat,
run your new knife under the bottom of your tongue,
then wander all night for a woman,
nose into her wind,
the skin rising in ridges along your back,
your whole life gambled on one last dance in a
    clearing,

trying to shake the stars out of your bones,
scatter them like embers on the ground,
wait for days, maybe weeks for someone to pick
    one up,
blow on it enough to bring you back to life.

River Gods

Sometimes they churn through rock,
then lie down in the beds
of the rivers they make,
their bodies still full of the sound of
moving water.

Sometimes they stop under the earth
and open their mouths
and those dark springs you see
in the forest begin to speak.

I have seen rivers turn countless times
and circle themselves,
I have seen rivers turn to ice overnight,
and rivers that come up out of their banks
and lie next to the bed,
and I have seen rivers leap into the veins of men,
their lives suddenly gone wild, misguided,
the river gods laughing somewhere
out in deep country
their hands brushing the earth
divining for water
44 as if it were blood.

A Last Poem: The Deaths of Fathers

It will certainly concern itself with light,
the way the light appeared on the morning of each
     death:
liquid, yellowed, frayed at the edges.

It will have something about rivers,
something about the beauty
of the way the bank holds the water,
how firmness knows enough to let something by
once in a while,
knowing it will come back,
settle in again.

This last poem will have something about the body,
about the bodies of sons in the late afternoons
of their fathers' deaths:
how all of them felt as if a shadow
had rended itself from the flesh,
walked away, turned
and through the distance of haze, waved,
not a signal of leaving,
but one which said:

"I will wait somewhere here on this other side
for your life to gather enough speed to cross over,"

and bending, each father will leave a sign,
some mark in the dust.

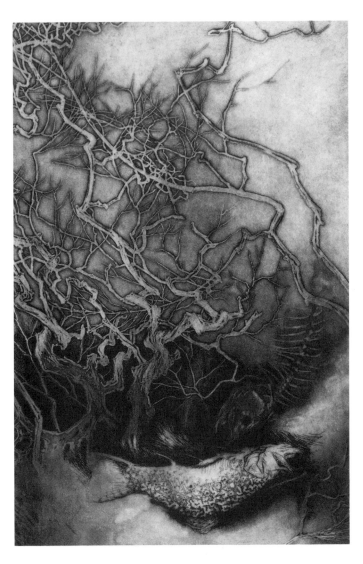

I catch exactly nothing, staring hard
for hours into the darkening current
that flows like light
from some extinguished star.

Nick Bozanic

Essays

Inner Fishing

Better than anything I know, trout fishing serves as a pause, a deep breath in the crush of living. It is a deceptive form of enlightenment: it seems incredibly simple, yet trout fishing illuminates an inner life, asks the mind and body to give themselves over to another power. It requires, as do most forms of enlightenment, a long period of careful study, pain and suffering, passion, a manic devotion to ritual, and the mastery of a series of subtle moves.

The long study for most trout fishermen means an entire childhood with only glimpses of trout streams. Instead, you are spirited off to bluegill ponds and given the traditional cane pole and bobber or an incredibly inexpensive Zebco rod and reel. You spend your first ten years digging for worms, trudging through tall grass in search of warm water ponds, and rowing the boat for your father. The trout stream is only a fantasy concocted out of the smells and images drifting out of your father's old fishing vest.

Initiation into the world of trout fishing comes subtly. At first, the old man is careful to let you only "touch" the bamboo rod. Later, he will let you land a fish or two, but always with his hands firmly wrapped around yours.

The novice enters the world of trouting as a heathen. Your hands are bloodied by the deaths of countless nightcrawlers and by the sure knowledge of how to hook a frog through the lips to catch bass. Salvation finally arrives at your twelfth or thirteenth Christmas. Your first flyrod, usually fiberglass and indestructible, weighs heavy in your hands. The reel is a single-action cheapy that looks good but is hardly a match for your father's lightweight heirloom. You borrow his rusty flies, or scoop them out of the wastebasket after they have been chewed to uselessness by huge fish.

Your movements on the stream are awkward, a ragged imitation of the master angler in your mind. You begin the long process of learning to read streams. Secrets are revealed in current patterns and in the way water piles up around rocks. There are early mornings filled with fog and mist, summers spent smelling cedar swamps and rain-swollen streams. You begin thinking, dreaming, talking constantly of trout.

Now begins the minute cataloging of stream details. You find a favorite stretch of water and fish it for weeks on end, carrying home new details to add to the imaginary stream you are building in your mind. Later, this dream-born trout stream will be complete, a place to retreat into and fish over and over. For now, you dissect, analyze, and at nineteen or twenty call yourself an angler.

After countless pairs of leaky waders you know well the cost in terms of human comfort: inhaling thousands of insects, learning to smoke lousy cigars to keep them away, and absorbing gallons of ice-cold rainwater. Too often you will spend twenty dollars on the wrong flies or find yourself stumbling along a river in the dark with a fly stuck in your forehead.

Yet the imaginary stream grows more detailed.

Without realizing it, when you are depressed, your mind takes you there. The water has become an old, familiar place and you watch yourself practice the correct presentation of the fly, putting all twenty-five or thirty years of your experience into the cast of the line.

In your quest for fishing mastery you will admit to being a manic fisherman. You wake in the middle of the night and check the calendar for the trout opener, check and recheck your gear, and spend more time with your wife so you can bargain for a few more minutes of being late in the summer. All your fishing movement is the observation of a perfectly contrived dance, a ritual each time you gather up your equipment and place it carefully in the car. This ritual takes on many forms. Perhaps a sip of whiskey before each outing, or tying leaders with two knots always in the same place. Perhaps it's the way you take the rod out of its case and push it together, gently, aiming the guides as though targeting an imaginary fish. The entire sequence becomes second nature, something to hand down to a son or daughter, something to give your life a kind of permanence and clarity.

At forty-five or fifty you feel you have mastered the sport. All the ritual and suffering, the intense passion of hooking and netting fish, accumulates on your inner stream. Each movement of the rod becomes a movement of your entire body. On those bright autumn days there is no difference between you and the stream. Even at home, when you add a small detail to the interior stretch of water, you feel the way your legs go numb in your waders. You have passed from a boy who merely wished for a fly to land somewhere near a fish to a bundle of sinew and nerves aimed not only at fishing, but also at the purity trout fishing offers.

So it is that, years later, when you finally give your equipment to a young disciple you will still be able to feel the tug of line in your arm. It all adds up, the study, pain, intense pleasure, practicing the ritual. We get where we are not by where we want to go or by where we've been, but by what we do with each moment. On the inner stream time ceases, for memory makes no distinction as to the coming and passing of seasons. The stream is always open, the slicks and runs exactly where you first started to construct them as a boy.

You stand on the edge of this mental flowing of water, slide in and take that first, quick breath in the

Steelhead Dreams

Tonight, just before I fall asleep, I hear the wind kick up in the red pines outside the house. I begin to go under, begin to submerge myself in a dream I know is waiting for me. "The steelhead run with the wind," I remember someone saying. And I think of thousands of fish gathering at the mouths of rivers up and down Lake Michigan. I begin to think of my bed and how I lie on top of it as some way I am able to hover just over the dream. As if the dream itself were made of water and I could lower myself down into a river choked with March ice. Holding. Just off a river mouth.

I listen. Underwater the wind sounds like thousands of waterfalls. A dull roar. A roar coming from far off and seeping gradually into my head. There are hundreds of fish waiting. They fan slowly, move up and down, some sideways in the current coming out of the river.

If I listen clearly enough to the inside of my head, I can hear the sound of some old command, some old memory let loose far upstream calling me in.

The water turns chemical. Chemicals loose in the tiny brains of these fish washing through their bodies, urging them upriver.

They surge through deadfall, upstream, rounding bends deep underwater, the sound of the river mixing with the sound of wind. All chemical. Something drifting now in their bodies. Bodies that look like pure aluminum muscles loose in the water.

First light. The fish stop just below the dam. The water moves past their eyes boiling with ice. In the steelhead dream I drift just off bottom. The bed, mattress, the room gone icy. I think I hear echoes in my head. The sound of rocks moving underwater. Fish moving against each other. Each fish noses into the current, settling toward bottom. My arms and wrists go limp in the dream, only a few hours left to rest here. Hold close to bottom. Pretend I know the way back. Pretend I can somehow rise back into my body, barely able to lift myself toward sunrise.

The fishermen move out of their houses hours before dawn. Maybe the river is twenty, thirty miles away. Or maybe they come from the cities, drive all night, migrating north.

In their cars, their heads begin to turn to steel. They imagine their arms and legs slowly churning to the color of slate blue. Their eyesight narrows. Their cars begin to swim through the darkness and when they stop to rest and step out into the night they believe the stars are the tiny points of hooks. They move farther north, not by watching the constellations, but by following the magnetic pull of steel forming in their heads. In their brains the cells are vibrating in close time with rivers. So close they hardly notice their bodies turning silver, their muscles taut, eyes running against the current of darkness flowing up over their hoods.

I send the line out thirty feet. "Steelhead run with the wind," Driscoll tells me. It drifts down the chute formed by the dam. I feel the lead weight bounce over gravel for twenty, perhaps thirty yards. Three minutes in the water and my feet go numb. Ice forms on my rod tip. I pull back slowly, hoping for a slight resistance, the mouth of a steelhead nosing my fly. Nothing.

Driscoll casts into the current. In four years, he has landed over three hundred steelhead. He tells me he fishes steelhead because it gives him some kind of balance. Fishing, he tells me, particularly steelhead fishing, has nothing to do with thinking. It is the balance between the cerebral, the meditative, and the physical. The biggest thing, he says, is the directness with which you catch a steelhead.

I have fished for trout for years. Never for steelhead. Mostly alone. Mostly in the early morning. Streamers laid out, then retrieved slowly. Meditative. Now, there are men upstream and down. Close. Packed in like fish. I cast perhaps forty times. Nothing.

Downstream men bunch together over the holes. They cast into the growing light. Suddenly, back near the dam a steelhead plunges upstream.

Someone's rod bends toward the water. The fish surges back downstream, then turns sideways against the current. The man holds. We pull our lines in. Everyone watches as he walks past us, holding the rod in close, bent almost double.

In the current the fish looks like a silver missile ripping upstream. Twenty minutes later he walks by, holding thirty inches of pure silver muscle, his fingers hooked under the gills.

He puts the fish on the stringer, ties it to an access fence pole, then goes back to fishing. I watch the fish fan slowly in shallow water.

We head home empty. I remember what Driscoll says about this sport. It's all in the drift, the length of your lead, the test line you use, and the weight and placement of split shot, he says. He tells me to walk the rivers, find out, he says, where the fish are and aren't, and then figure out why they aren't.

We go out another night. Fish the "rope hole" on the Platte River out of an old duck-hunting canoe. Forty degrees and raining/snowing, the wind ripping into my parka. "Steelhead run with the wind," he says again. We break several lines, casting again and again under the influence of mercury vapor lights from nearby cabins. Nothing.

I begin to think about this kind of fishing. Begin to think of the sheer numbers of fishermen standing next to each other at the Homestead Dam, and the sport turns narcotic. I begin to realize that the steelhead is in the brain. It runs deep, cuts down through the medulla, cerebellum, runs like a vein directly down the spinal column.

We leave again with nothing. On the way home I imagine the road to be a kind of river. I am guiding the truck directly into driving rain and snow. Both of us sit encased in steel. Steelhead fishermen. Driving home. Empty. Behind us the steelhead surge and circle at the river mouth. The truck fishtails through slush. A truck made of steel. Heads of steel. And on the hood: ice clinging to steel.

Casting: A Meditation

Something pushes me out the door and into foul weather. If pressed to identify the force, I might realize it comes from the throbbing in my temples, the beast of sitting in too many meetings. Or it might be the grip a nightmare life has on my imagination that makes me head for the river.

It is almost dark. Cold. Bits of rain and snow are falling. After five minutes in the water my hands stiffen, the wind rising to a low moan. I begin the ritual I've followed for over twenty years. No mantra here, only the rhythmic swish of my line cutting through the weather. I've casted this way for hours, years if you added them all up, and now, I find myself casting nowhere in particular to no fish in particular. Just casting. For all I know, with this collection of bad dreams festering in my head, I could be fishing for old tires. No matter. When it gets completely dark, I'm still at it, the line invisible now as it lifts and sings through the air.

I begin thinking to myself about the nature of the line, asking what it's really doing out there in the dark. If it were finer, longer, I might be able to loft it straight up into the sky, sew the constellations together. Make that direct link between Sagitarius and the North Star I've felt since birth.

Though fully awake after casting for hours, numbed by cold and repetition, I lapse into ever-specific waking dreams: out in front of me there surely is a raft of beautiful women, or maybe a bag of money floating downstream. Or I'll feel a heavy strike and miraculously recover some lost part of myself.

Finally, it comes to me that I'm really casting into the nothing of this northern Michigan night to get rid of something. Each curl of my wrist and I cast out a personal demon. Each cast and the bills and debts fall away, the car that won't start begins to vanish. But what I sense is that I can let the demons sulk there at the end of my line for only so long, then I must bring them back.

So I cast and retrieve, cast and retrieve, long into the night, praying for the line to come from deep inside me, from some pit in my belly where emptiness lives. I think of the millions of empty casts I've made, and here in the darkness they suddenly start coming back, crisscrossing over me like a net, the sky luminous, clouds meshing over the moon, each cast a vein into memory.

Later, I try to fall asleep in the cabin, my casting arm throbbing under my pillow, and all the memories of my life on the water start sifting back into my hands. I think of the very heart of casting: not how I cast, but why. I think of the metaphorical beauty of empty casts, the dark edge of faith honed by the resignation of coming up empty almost every time. And I think of how the act of casting has linked me to the men I honor. I remember my grandfather calling back over his shoulder from the front of the boat just before a lightning storm on Turk Lake. "Keep casting," he whispers. "Cast for all you're worth." "Cast your heart out," he said, and I remember how he once told me that every time he made a cast he felt part of himself go free. So I cast there with him in the dream, our rhythm perfect. He stands in the bow, casting under the lightning, the bass cruising like phantoms under the boat, his rod etched with light.

Brook Trout

It begins this way: my head is tight, worn down from a month of hundred-degree days in the worst drought of South Carolina's history. A month of teaching as a writer-in-residence at a conservative Baptist university. Three strikes, I think: the South, a city in the South, and heat in the South beyond control.

So I find, after two weeks at home in northern Michigan, some distant memory drifting in my melted synapses of how to go brook trout fishing.

On the map I look north into Traverse Bay, safe in the knowledge the fat boys from the cities are trolling deep for salmon and lake trout.

Brook trout. I haze over. The map turns all green and I trace a line from my house into the woods near Nessen City where the Little Betsie River trickles from a swamp.

After I put on an old green corduroy shirt I slip twenty dollars into the breast pocket and head along the southern edge of Green Lake, the twenty resting easy. Nothing to buy. No real destination except fishing.

Fly fishing for brook trout. And I hit the edge of the gravel and slide into a long corridor of huge oak trees. At the first bridge two delinquents from Detroit are drifting the ends of night crawlers into a deep pool. If I had a gun I would at least pat it next to my shoulder holster just to make sure.

I drive on, turning west into a private but unused drive, and get out, the music of Jimmy Buffet trailing behind me. At streamside the full impact of fishing in dense brush sets in.

There is nothing except brush and swamp between me and towns like Nessen City, Copemish, and

59

Kaleva. A few more or less human beings. So I start casting and think about where I am. High in the hand of Michigan. I am in generally lawless country, Benzie County, and I am fishing in a wild place. I cast to the best spots: up against deadfall, tag alder.

In the hour three fish come gently into my hand. Brook trout for breakfast. I tell myself each time I take the life of a brook trout it might be possible for those tiny specks of color to get into my bloodstream, explode some morning, my life turning luminous.

So I drive home, the brook trout iced down in the small cooler. Five miles down the road I pull over and run my hands over their slick sides. They feel like they are covered in silk, and the movement of my hand is the same movement I use to caress a woman's leg.

I stop in Interlochen, buy a beer. Several more. I treat the bar in a celebration of brook trout weather and punch in six old songs on the juke box on my way out the door.

Looking down at the fish next to me in the seat, I half believe the talisman I carry: the small leather bag filled with sweetgrass, three pieces of red pine from the Upper Peninsula carved into bears' teeth, a rock from Lake Superior with a hole through the middle. Everything comes down to this: fishing and three brook trout in the seat next to me, the dreams I had in July of wandering in South Carolina heat, bending to a stream, and then, somehow, the ice cold shock of old Michigan water. Brook trout loose in the water. Brook trout and the water inside the brook trout. Brook trout cells passing through me, my heart pumping the bloodstream where invisible particles of Michigan, brook trout, and glacial water rest and lodge in the delicate curves of my veins.

60

Fly Fishing: A Consideration

I must confess, since I learned to fish at the age of two, I have fished in fresh water with almost everything imaginable: crayfish, worms, bread balls, BB guns, a Labatt's can outfitted with treble hooks for pike in Canada, live grasshoppers, frogs hooked through the lips for bass, jigs, spoons, plugs, cowbells, fish parts, and once, in a fit of confusion, I tried to hook a particularly obnoxious Chihuahua on a dock in front of an Au Sable cabin so I could use it for a large moth imitation.

True, this is not a list of baits and lures most fly fishermen would own up to, but I mean to offer as admissible evidence the fact that I know some of the extremes of fishing. Raised a bait fisherman who spent hour after hour in pursuit of pike, bass, and bluegills with my father, I was introduced early to fly fishing. Now, when I look back and think of him casting out over the old green rowboat on bass lake for bedding "gills," I remember how I ached to use his old bamboo fly rod. And when I moved north, that rod came with me.

For the last twenty years fly fishing has been on my list of the top two things to do with your time. Surely, fly fishing is spiritually linked to making love: both require delicacy, passion, finesse, and, above all, accuracy. Fly fishing and making love can, if left unchecked, become an obsession. I have squandered hundreds of dollars over the years thinking that I could tempt the god of fishing up close with expensive gear and the "right" flies. Surely, over the same period I have spent an equal amount on perfume, dinners, and Victoria's Secret orders.

61

All the good arguments have been made for the upper hand which fly fishing holds in the imaginations of fishermen: it's a quiet pursuit, often in the cleanest water you can find, and is best done alone. Perhaps the best way to come to some real understanding about the virtues of fly fishing is to compare it to something on the other end of the spectrum. Anyone who has spent time on a salmon or steelhead stream knows that Tom McGuane is right: one of the primary requirements for catching a lake-run rainbow or salmon is a room-temperature I.Q.

Walk a salmon stream after the season and you'll find mile after mile of debris: beer cans, tangles of forty-pound line, cheap wine bottles, and an occasional mud-splattered *Hustler* magazine. A northern Michigan salmon stream is a good place to round up escapees both mental and criminal, and surely parts of the crowd who line these streams include armed thugs, psychopaths, and general public nuisances. In short, spending time on a salmon stream, where the population density is often equal to that of Los Angeles, is not a nice activity. It's where brutality and a lack of civility get you farther than a college degree.

Not true on a trout stream, at least a trout stream which honors the old etiquette established hundreds of years ago: fly fishermen are generally very social people. If you run into a fellow fly fisherman he will almost always engage you in polite conversation. Nothing nosy. You don't have the sensation that the man across the stream from you has a Bowie knife in his back pocket or that he is out on bail. Nor do you feel the tremendous anxiety and frenzy associated with the "meat packing" mentality of many salmon fishermen. On the other hand many fly fishermen catch and release, only occasionally taking one home for the fire. And certainly catch and release is fine high moral ground to walk, but nothing is better for the soul than a broiled brook trout and a single red potato, white wine, and, afterward, a beautiful woman reaching for your casting arm.

Fly fishing goes well beyond being a superior form of fishing for perhaps hundreds of reasons, one of them being the very nature of the activity. Fishing with a fly takes you to the very heart of predator/prey activity. Any good hunter or fisherman has, at the heart of his pursuit, respect for what he's after. This is where fly fishing takes the off-ramp into the uncharted regions of beauty and peace. All you really need to do to sense what it's like to be alone on a trout stream in the middle of the night, the only sound coming from your line swishing the air, is to listen for several hours to Esther Lamandier sing, and let her voice be a reminder that what is lovely is sometimes tangible. It isn't hard to imagine her half-clothed, casting some-where under a French moon, the line invisible, her body pressed against the current.

When you step back from watching Babe Winkle-man haul in yet another northern pike on a lure that looks like half a Cadillac, or bump into one too many nitwits from Georgia salmon fishing on the Manistee, men who have obviously graduated from the "Ted Nugent Casting School," it's exalting to know that fly fishing immediately transports you out of the world of crass, "catch 'em and club 'em" mentality into a universe of refinement. Fly fishing is a world where you might well encounter someone toting a bottle of Dom Perignon, rather than a six of Blatz.

So whether it's attempting to present a size eighteen Hendrickson to a brook trout on still water, or lifting the edge of your wife's blouse without detection, the mind works the same: move slowly, handle every-thing like it was made of the most delicate, sacred skin. And when you make contact, respect the wild-ness that surges through every fiber of your self. When it's over, rest. Commit yourself to a lifetime of this. Give yourself over to it every chance you get.

63

Out for Blood

There is the strain of sitting in the fighting chair of a large ocean craft, strapped into a fishing harness, a kind of mini-straightjacket, your arms turned to jelly against a huge marlin. And there is the contrasting joy of sitting in a rowboat, drinking beer and casting plugs under a full moon for bass. But there is something about salmon fishing that takes you into the realms of philosophy and religion: standing chest deep in a river watching the movements of hundreds of fish, all on their spawning run upstream where they will mate and eventually die. And you're out there, standing in a river that is at once alive and surging with fish and again is like standing in water that flows directly from the mouth of death.

Give me September and October off work and a supply of hard currency and I'd head for certain points on the globe where salmon fishing is at its most refined: Iceland, Nova Scotia, New Brunswick, but above all, Scotland. I'd spend lots of cash to fish in Scotland, on the Spey River where you can rent a section of river called a "beat" and fish under the watchful eye of a ghillie, or guide, and hook salmon after salmon. And at night, back at the inn, you have your fish cooked for you, all the while sipping whiskey that you swear has boiled up from the ground itself.

Salmon fishing in such exquisite places as Scotland is done under ritualistic, prescribed conditions. There are rules and expectations set forth by your fellow anglers. You have to know how to act and you have to act according to very old traditions handed down by generations of fishermen. And if you've caught the legendary fish that your ghillie has told you has hung under the bank for a decade or so, then you become the legend itself. After you leave, your name will sift through conversations for years. Reverence. A kindly Scottish nod toward all the skill and patience you so aptly displayed.

In Scotland you're not out for meat, necessarily, but to honor the tradition of salmon fishing and its sport, often using expensive, hand-made two-handed bamboo fly rods, equally expensive reels, all the while dressed to the hilt with an oiled cotton jacket and a tie, of all things. But there are other places in the world where you come to find that the word "beat" takes on literal interpretations, particularly when it comes to salmon fishing in northern Michigan.

If you are about to go salmon fishing in northern Michigan, forget any pastoral notions of fishing, forget Scotland and all its finesse. Forget the modicum of civility you found on the chalk streams of England or the blue-ribbon rivers of New England. Northern Michigan salmon fishing is the equivalent of electroshock therapy. And for the purposes of analogy, salmon fishing in other areas of the world, particularly Scotland, is like being hooked up to the electrodes by a woman of refinement, say Beverley Sills, the wondrous opera singer, while up here, our kind of fishing, north of the forty-fifth parallel, is more akin to having Madonna jump start you with a car battery.

What we're talking about here is fishing for blood, meat, salmon that have come from the water of Lake Michigan to spawn and die, but not before you've had your chance at them.

And forget the good life on the way over. There are no stops for caviar or cognac in crystal snifters. At best, if you stop at Johnnies Log Cabin Bar outside of Honor you can get a draft and a shot of Yukon Jack, then sift through the smoke for a woman to whet your appetite for fishing. And you'll likely find her: large, robust, a local, the kind of woman who would gladly cradle your head between her thighs and then crack it like an egg.

This is beer territory. A place where a college degree is a serious liability. A region of the upper Midwest where you are probably surrounded by all kinds of outlaws, poachers, lumberjacks on the lam, and more con men than on any corner in New York. It's desperate here, and so is this kind of fishing.

Even before you get to the river you need to get your head ready to face a veritable gauntlet: men, most of them drunk and too many from out of state, who have loaded themselves up with flagons of alcohol and the most crass equipment possible. Normally you would fish for salmon with an exquisite bamboo fly rod, a hand-tied salmon fly, and a head full of reverence for the angling tradition you're about to enter into. Not so on the salmon streams up here.

Your first reaction after pulling onto the shoulder to park is that you'll need some kind of weapon to fight through the crowds. And you're dead right. There are lots of out-of-state plates, vans, big four-wheelers with cofee mugs on the dashboards driven by the locally unemployed. Your first step into the swamp path back to the stream puts you headed for trouble.

At the river you'll likely meet up with large groups of drunken tourist-come-fishermen disguised as natives, many from such unlikely places as Georgia or Louisiana, where they haven't ever seen a salmon. From here, the vision of lots of men stomping up and down along the river gets worse.

There's no room here for high-dollar equipment, delicate rods, oiled cotton jackets, and sporty hats. These guys mean business. They fish, not with flies, which are the legal means of hooking fish, but with large and illegal treble hooks, three nasty pitch-fork-looking contraptions wired together, twenty-pound monofilament line, and brutishly thick rods that most of them use at home to pull their engines and transmissions.

66

Their methods are equally brutal: they don't cast and retrieve, cast and retrieve, the usual method of putting the lure to the fish, working the fly with the deft touch of a magician, an act of meditation. Instead, what they do with their treble hooks tied to lead weights the size of small anchors is more akin to dredging. Similar, I would say, to the way the Coast Guard drags for bodies. They usually cast up above the salmon pools and then rip down through the bottoms of them, often foul hooking fish and then hauling them up on the bank. Great sport for city dwellers and those with football-score I.Q.s, most of whom have driven for hours in search of easy meat, not sentiment and reflection, the nether side of fishing.

At other sites along the river the story is the same. When you step into the line of over a hundred men along the bank and begin casting, you've essentially said you're in for the duration. If someone hooks a fish and says "Fish-On" then everyone takes their line out of the water, the fisherman walks past, lands his fish and then immediately walks back to the spot he held before he caught the fish. Pecking order. Pissing order. If you get in someone's spot, you pay.

I have seen men driven up against their cars by other fishermen wielding tire irons all because they stepped into the wrong spot in line. And I have seen men bloody each other over hooked fish and I have seen men chase salmon out of the water and up onto dry land, then gaff them for the broiling pan.

My own tastes, largely fed by years of fly fishing for trout, a more delicate art, have me on the stream when almost everyone is either too drunk to continue, or exhasted from keelhauling so much meat on a given day. For me, fishing is a pursuit steeped in ritual and reflection. Robert Traver, perhaps the finest of angling writers, once wrote that his fishing was "an endless source of delight and an act of small rebellion." Quite simply, I fish because it takes me into a world where I am the predator. Even though I mostly practice catch and release fishing I honor the practice of taking game or wild food from the environs where I live. The poet Gary Snyder invokes this necessity as a way to keep some sense of the wild in ourselves. And wild, I feel, when I am fishing alone.

I often stand in the failing light and wait for a salmon pool to fill with spawning fish. I have seen four or five hundred at a time in a pool the size of an old Desoto. Most evenings I'll cast a delicate nymph pattern and let it drift along the bottom, waiting for the strike at the end of the drift. Then the slight lift and the fish is hooked.

The reel hums and vibrates and the hooked salmon moves like lightning in this small stream. I'll fight the fish for ten or fifteen minutes and then bring it to my hand, exhausted. For an instant there is that predatory instinct and I dispatch the fish, as they say, with a "priest," really a darkly polished walnut club handed down from generations of fishermen. After that, I watch the fish fade, first from bright silver to a dull grey.

Once a year I go into the swamp alone. I fish all night. And I remember a few things. I remember that in front of this very pool I am fishing I have watched men haul up salmon like old boots, beat them and rise from the banks with their hands bloody, and then another pass of their hooks and they are at it again.

68   When I hook my last fish I bring him into the gentle arc of lantern light. Pure silver pulsing, spent there in the dark. And just before I begin to clean him I think of those old photos of the salmon ritual from the Northwest Indian tribes: the chief wearing a suit made entirely out of salmon skins. The bounty of salmon nourishing a tribe, an entire way of life, right thinking. Even though the fish dies quickly, it still quivers there in my hands, its nerves flashing like distant stars.

Then I begin the same ritual I have followed for years. No chants, but the awareness that I am about to extinguish the life of a fish to enrich my own: one cut and I find the heart. Tiny. Glistening there in my hand like a large ruby. And every fall I eat the raw heart of one salmon, then I cook the fish in the dark of the swamp and wait for the darker night to surround the fire. Call it ritual. Call it a need to eat something entirely wild. Call it an act of desperation, but there is something in the heart of salmon that asks death to wait a little longer at the door. And there is something equally insistent that eating this fish alone in the dark of the swamp, far from the supermarket, far from shrink-wrapped, force-fed meat, arranged like rows of shoes, is, finally, a way to keep the soul engines running on spirit rather than commerce and cash.

On the way home I pass the vans still parked on the road. Quiet now, most of the men asleep, passed out, the smell of fish and beer and piss mixed in the bushes. All the way home I feel the ache in my arm of casting, hooking fish, a night of salmon exhaustion in my forearm. And I feel each beat of my heart. Steady. Rhythmic. A man with two hearts, one his own, the other: salmon. And all the way home I dream myself into a suit made entirely of salmon skins and I feel a new pulse: how the wild salmon heart hammers inside my chest while my own heart cups the blow.

River gods

You may have heard this story. Maybe a long time ago. Maybe it was in a little cafe with a few old calendars askew on the walls, some gut-busting eggs frying on the back griddle. But when you heard it, you knew it was legend.

It was a story about going to the river every spring. He was almost sixty the last time he did it, he said. He had fished the same water for five decades with his grandfather and his father. They called it their water. The rituals were carried out meticulously each season: opening-day breakfast, checking the gear, exchanging small presents, then the walk to the river. And after both of them had died, he kept a secret, he said, something he always did in private, always at the same spot where the creek fed into the mainstream.

He had borrowed this, he was saying. Borrowed this part of his own private ritual from an aborigine tribe in Australia. It was something about respect, about giving yourself over. He always used the same knife, he said, and pulled an old Boy Scout jackknife out of his front pocket.

Then he showed the motion he used. Not a quick slice over his wrist but a slow, delicate draw over his forearm. Then he pulled up his sleeve and the scars laced his arm. Each one small, distinct, his left forearm covered with inch-long memories.

The bleeding never lasted long, he said. Just long enough to let a little blood fall into the river. He'd mix it slowly with his hand, then wave it along. He never said anything, only watched the way the blood swirled into the clear water, then dissolved, disappeared, became river. Twenty seasons. Twenty cuts.

70

After he left, I looked at my own smooth forearm, thought of the rivers I knew, the dream rivers I fished in my sleep, rivers full of mermaids, phantoms. And that day, after I heard his story, I found an old Barlow knife my father had given me at Hartwick Pines and cleaned it up.

It was there in the basement, halfway into early morning, that I felt the edge, honed perfectly. And I thought about the small gods who bless rivers, the ones who bless our fishing lives, the ones who bless our hands, the ones who bless each drop of water. I thought of my life somehow transported into each one of their favors. I thought of heading out in April, through early mist, perhaps the apparitions of ghost relatives, or the visions of waking dreams, lining the path to the river. I knew the exact spot near the Au Sable over a pure spring where I would kneel down, roll up my sleeve, and make the cut, begin the process of giving myself over.

Boat Dreams

In my efforts to trace my development as a fly fisherman I always end up in the same place: watching my father cast for bluegills with a beat-up Horrocks & Ibbottson bamboo fly rod off the bow of an old green rowboat. Since then, I've not owned many boats. When I was in high school my father and I built a *Popular Mechanics* "Mini-Most" hydroplane from marine plywood in our basement on High Street. We still laugh about how we never figured how we'd get it *out* of the basement, but we did, and I raced all summer, crash throttle and all. Other boat memories inevitably collect, like iron on a magnet, around the first really beautiful boat I ever saw.

My father and I were fishing a lake near Greenville and had borrowed a boat which belonged to his boss, Walt Emery. He was an old-style woodsman: he built lean-tos and slept on pine boughs, drank coffee from old blue-flecked tin cups, and never washed his dishes. And he had a boat. One beautiful, handmade Penn Yan made from strips of cedar covered with canvas. I remember lifting it with my father for the first time, its lightness somehow born of air itself. When we put it on the water and got in, I remember how the wood gave under my feet, how the ribs of the boat moved when we moved.

Walt's boat was silent in the water, a boat that you could, as McGuane says, "pole in dew." It drew less than a half-inch of water and slipped up on lilly pads like a cloud. It was green, a cascade medium green, and the insides were a kind of luminous brown, the patina of years of use and care radiating up out of the grain.

I left that boat at Walt Emery's thirty years ago and have wanted one since. I know there are those who will tell you that fortune is something you have to seek, but my fortunes have come mostly by blind luck. Just two weeks ago a friend called who had once offered me a chance to buy a boat just like Walt Emery's. When the offer was made, I had no money. This time the price was right: a steal on a fourteen-foot Thompson cedar boat. Handmade. When I said I'd take it over the phone, Walt Emery's boat suddenly began to re-form in my imagination.

Now the Thompson is moored in front of the house. It's green. A deep brown spar varnished color inside. Some nights I go out on the lake and lie down, my ribs against the ribs of this boat, and when I breathe I can feel the boat moving with me. This is a boat that defies the world as it is. It's old, an antique from the late forties. It wasn't stamped out of a sheet of recycled cans in a factory, and it doesn't make noise like an aluminum boat. It requires care and patience, both of short supply in my life. A therapy boat. A boat to build a summer of guiding for bluegills around. A boat to get lost in, every day for months on end.

For now, this boat represents big plans. I'll fish out of it for the next forty years, rising early to cast streamers, or simply row out with my daughter to see the night sky one more time. And there will be a last night: I'll row out with my wife, beg her for one last natural act and then send her over the side to swim for home. Me? I'll douse myself and the boat with gasoline and let the whole thing go, Viking style. They can find what's left at the bottom.

From the house, when I look down at my boat I can only thank the one or two people who put it together with brass screws and glue in Peshtigo, Wisconsin, when Truman was president. And I'm sure that some night I'll go down to the water and find myself sitting

The Legacy of Worms

To a fly fisherman who has an inflated opinion of himself and his fraternity, nothing is quite as loathesome as a worm fisherman. Perhaps, because of the media attention over the years to the "purity" of fly fishing, worming has gotten some bad ink. I must confess to a certain snobbishness at times. After all, who am I kidding when I step into the Au Sable with a thousand dollars worth of Orvis gear. I'm fishing. I'm worthy of practicing deception. I've got the stuff to prove it: fly boxes, graphite rods, tiny gadgets with the right logo. But this is all fakery. We all know, when we drool over equipment, that somehow, beyond this world of high-tech boron-graphite fibers, underneath all this foppery, there is instinct.

Maybe it was instinct that told me to get up early with my father to go looking for worms. He knew the best places: under leaves, cool and moist. Or we went out late at night on the summer lawn, feeling in the dark for crawlers, remembering later how they slipped like greased sausages through our fingers. Even now, from a distance of thirty years, I can still hear the sound they made when they plunked into the wet leaves and dirt at the bottom of a rusty Hills Brothers worm can.

If fishing is about anything for me, it is about recollection, the way my mind has of letting itself unravel and hook around the sensation that the dead are surely watching us from the banks or are standing on shore measuring each cast. Inevitably, when I think of ancestors and fishing I go back to Bass Lake and my grandfather's cottage. I go back to fishing with live bait, almost always worms, any kind of worm we could find. Back then, in the fifties, I learned the secret techniques from my father and grandfather about how to think of the hook as a kind of needle, the worm as fabric, the whole rig set up to keep the worm alive as long as possible, moving, imagining its slow dance underwater.

And the ghosts are always there when I fish now. I can see my grandfather baiting up for perch using tiny red worms, or my father and me anchored just off a deserted island, how we sifted through the can of crawlers for the patriarch of all worms, the one that felt lucky. Then he'd break one in half and spit on it and I'd make that long cast toward the lily pads, waiting for the bass to explode up out of the weeds.

There are other visions, some taken from my father's stories, and always they are visions of ritualistic, nearly sacred value: men hunched over hooks in the rain, mumbling old fishing prayers, invocations carried on the souls of countless worms. But the most stunning image is one passed on about one of my fater's old fishing buddies from the forties, Fred Lewis, and how he must have looked when he turned toward a question just after baiting up, the hook in his teeth, and a gob of nightcrawlers dribbling down the side his mouth.

Now, each year, maybe out of respect for the dead, maybe out of superstition, before I set my gear up, before I get out my hundred-and-fifty-dollar fly reels, the flashy graphite rods, the Wheatley fly boxes, I go into my study and take out the bandana in which I have wrapped the talismans of my life. A power stone from Lake Superior is hidden in there, and a lovely handmade Chinese fish given as a gift by an equally lovely student. Perhaps most powerful of all, there are bits and pieces of what's left from my grandfather's tackle: misshapen sinkers, rusted hooks, used crawler harnesses, the stuff of fishing a lifetime with worms.

The old men come back each winter, singly and in pairs, numbers diminishing with time, to reclaim their rivers.

Harmon Henkin

Stories

Barth's Water

This would have been a good day for Barth. He loved the way the gray clouds scudded in from the north, dipped low, and mixed with the mist and fog rising off the river. These were his days and he liked to call me early enough so we could come to this spot on the river, build a small fire, and drink whiskey from the old, blue-flecked tin cups we kept hidden near the fire pit. Three or four times each August Barth and I knew the bone-deep joy of sitting in the cold gray dawn with nothing planned. We saved these days, counted them in the long string of time we wanted to add to our memories, knowing someday we would total them up, proclaiming to each other we had known and shared a fine degree of satisfaction.

We had known this particular bend for well over twenty years, fishing for weeks at a time, always stopping just below the feeder stream where the bank rose to a slight, grassy hump. We were friends in the way two men who have shared a lot in their lives are friends. Barth had given me a good deal of his fishing knowledge. I grew with him, entering my thirties under his tutelage, listening to his raw-edged voice telling me how to know the river.

Barth was a deeply patient man, made wise by years of constant observation and quiet reflection. His face betrayed the seasonal changes of living sixty-five years in Michigan. Leaning close, you could see the ice-blue water of Lake Superior in his eyes, sense what it meant to stand in a full-force November gale on the big lake, the wind trying to rip the skin from your face. Yet, there was a softness in him. Somewhere in the lines around his eyes were the remnants of cool summer nights spent in the north. His complexion glowed that deep ruddy color the skin takes on only after it has been exposed to year after year, season after season, of snow and rain: sixty-five years of facing into the weather.

Today, Barth was not with me. I measured the river with my eyes as the stone-colored mist seeped out of the trees and passed away in front of me. Then I felt in my pack for the box Barth had given me five years earlier. It was made of pine and the joints were perfectly dove-tailed, smoothed exquisitely by years of handling and rubbing. That night, five years ago, he poked it at me while we sat in this same spot. "Here," he said, "hang onto this until I give you something to put in it." I held it for a moment, then lifted the cover and read the inscription, which had been scrawled on a plain piece of paper and pasted on the inside: "For Jonas Barth, from his father, March, 1931."

"A gift," he said. "My father made that box in the middle of the Depression. When I was a kid, growing up, that box meant everything to me. It was one of the few things I had which I could call my own. I kept a silver dime in it I found at the circus. Then, it held a picture of my mother and father and after that a wedding ring. If you smell it, there's a faint odor of lilac. My mother grew them outside her kitchen window, and each spring she'd give me a little sprig to keep inside. Just hang onto it for me."

After that night, Barth mentioned the box only once. That was his way of doing things. He never talked more than necessary and I knew any reference to the gift would be met with a blank stare and his soft smile.

I put the box away and forgot about it until one night this May when Barth gave me an envelope. "That's my will. Take it home tonight and read through it. Let me know what you think."

At first I wanted to ask the obvious question, but his face stopped the words in my throat. I sensed his need for me to remain silent and we spent a good deal of that night just sipping from the cups.

For the next several nights of fishing I waited for Barth to ask my opinion, but he never did. For a week we fished and drank and I sensed an urgency in his movements I had not known. His eyes seemed to deepen, and our conversations became opportunities for Barth to pass on little-known facts and tricks about fishing. He used the time to let me know that I was a man who was being subtly gifted with more than a friendship. On one of our last nights together he leaned close to fill my cup and, in his characteristic style, handed me a crumpled piece of yellow paper, a list of all his gear. "The will doesn't mean as much as this does. Just put the ashes in the box I gave you. Pick a day you think I'd like and just let them go here." There was no emotion in his voice, and he was as sure and strong as I had ever known him to be.

"Aren't you rushing things a bit? You're only sixty-five."

"Sixty-five is more than enough time to do what I've wanted to do. Just give an old man his rest, then go back to the house and gather up all my gear and get what use you can out of it."

I began to speak again, but he thrust the bottle toward me as if to say, "That's it, just keep things simple." For the rest of the night neither of us spoke much. I watched him as he watched the fire. His face changed in the firelight. Barth was a river man, and as we sat there listening to the water trail away from us I could see he had arrived at a great acceptance. I knew better than to question him, and occasionally he looked across at me and nodded the way he did when he knew you understood.

That was two months ago. Barth died in July. It was a painless death, the kind most men wish for. A death in the middle of the night, asleep and submerged deep in a dream. His daughter flew in from California and

83

had him cremated. Afterward she gave me the ashes and I put them in the box, just as Barth had wanted.

What brought me here this morning felt like a gentle tug in my imagination. I carried the box outside, put it in my pack, and walked the mile and a half to the river. At first the fog was too thick and I could only smell and hear the river. I sat down near the old fire pit and piled a tiny bit of kindling. The smoke curled upward around my face, hovered for a moment, then rose into the mist. I was thinking about Barth and the years he spent teaching me this section of the river. He wanted to make sure I knew it well enough to call each bend and pool back to him in my memory. This was Barth's water and he wanted me to know its finest runs and deepest pools. Now they were my runs and my pools.

I poured myself a cup of whiskey from the flask, then took out the box and lifted the cover. Slowly, I ran my fingers through the ashes, noticing that, like the day, they were a soft gray-white. On the bank I hesitated for a moment, then let them fall. They stayed only an instant on the surface, disappearing into the leaden water.

I thought of myself, a man caught up in the memory of another man, then drew in a deep breath of mist. I reached down and swirled the water and the last trace of ashes drifted away. Then my hand rose numb and cold, working itself around the flecks of an old tin cup.

The Elder

He made the agreement the first time all five of them were together. It seemed easy and innocent enough. He hadn't expected they would all die before him and he would have the cabin to himself. But he was alone, sitting on the porch in the sun, looking through his feet propped up on the railing.

The cabin was on a horseshoe bend on the North Branch, and in between sips of whiskey he looked up and down the river for some sign of insect activity. But his mind drifted, and he spent a good deal of the afternoon remembering how all five of them had gathered each June at the judge's, drank and played cards, and fished a little. He was the youngest, but eighteen years before, when they had made the pact, they all joked that because of the way he lived, fishing and carousing around like a madman, he would be the first to go.

Now, everything was his. The tack room, where a fine old print of a rising rainbow hung over the beds, was stuffed with the best gear. He knew where each reel was stored and anticipated the feel of the judge's creel in his hands.

But there was another prize he had held in his 85 memory for years. The Dickerson rod had never been fished. It had been passed around each June, and each person would rub a drop of sour mash whiskey into the finish. All their names had been inscribed on it over the years, and they used to joke about who would finally get to use it.

For a while he stayed on the porch, felt the sun glance off the heavy rock chimney behind him. He wanted to go inside, take the rod out and lay it on the table, then open one of the bottles of George Dickle and annoint the rod by himself. But each time he tried to stand he fell back, not drunk, but weak, not from age, but from a lack of purpose.

Finally, when he could stand the cold no longer, he rose and took his forty-five years of sinew and bone into the tack room and found the rod. There had been three of them left in the spring. Two had died the previous year, and the three left, he, the judge, and the doctor, railed on into the night telling stories of huge fish, boats filled with water, and the way Dean changed his clothes in the middle of the river.

It had been a freak, he thought, for the judge and the doctor to die in the same year. He held the rod up to the light, smelled the odor of whiskey on its surface.

When he sat down at the table he sensed the coldness of the room. He wanted to hear them all laughing, throwing cards down on the table, scattering piles of dollar bills on the floor. Instead, he heard only the river rustling outside.

He drank heavily into the night. He watched the stars come out, the fog sift up out of the river and into the sky, then drank one more glass, straight, without ice.

Just before he left, he checked each room, made sure everything was where it had always been. He straightened the prints on the bedroom walls, closed the fishing books on the table, and walked into the living room.

He sat in the middle of the floor in darkness, the rod resting in his lap. For a while he ran his hands up and down the cane, feeling the black ink of each name fill in his fingertips. Then, in two swift motions, he rose and broke the rod into pieces.

He crumpled a piece of newspaper on the floor, then arranged the broken rod over it in tepee fashion. One swig of whiskey went down his throat and the bottom of the bottle he drained over the rod pieces.

He sat holding the match for a moment, looked into the flame, the shadows drifting over the walls, then touched the paper.

On the way up the hill he turned once, saw the cabin blazing below him, the reflection shooting up and down the river, then walked the rest of the way to the road. For a while he sat in the car, conscious only of the way the warmth he felt in his back disappeared into the seat.

The House

The river moved past the house in a long, slow arc as if it were sweeping a hand up over the bank. Inside at night when the man lay down he would fall asleep, imagining the river might slide in through the doors, washing through the rooms, and he would wake from a dream of floating sure he had felt the river in his bed. To him the river had become a place where the spirit of a beautiful woman slept during the day and moved into him in the darkness. And sometimes when restless and troubled he would walk from his room to the river and dip his hand for a moment to drink, the house rising dark and motionless behind him, the windows reflecting specks of starlight.

It was not his house in the beginning. On the ground where he stood he had heard stories of an Indian camp, then a trapper's shack, and finally the land sold at auction in Saginaw. The house was built from timber and glass and stone and looked as if the builder had walked to the river each day and pulled raw wood and rock from the sleeping arms of some spirit in the river.

The man from Saginaw had seemingly known this spirit, and the house gradually took on a combination of his character and the way his imagination began to see the bend in the river as a slight curve in the small of her back. There were places in the beams where you could still feel the tight fit between roof and wall, where the hands of a craftsman had made a pefect cut, the wood slipping together, interlocking like fingers. And each room held old fishing prints, or books, and to walk into this house was like walking into the soul of the man from Saginaw. And to lie down in this house was to fall asleep drifting into long arms, long hair, a woman's mouth dreaming toward your own.

After he sold, the man left his gear in the tack room. His fly bench and tools hung in their original positions, and there were flies of all sizes and colors, special patterns known only to this particular mile of frontage on the North Branch. There was a secret box of flies left in a drawer, a small green fly made to fish on the surface or deep in the face of the woman he had seen in dreams.

On this night when he had walked down to the bank with the Saginaw man's memory, he turned and looked into the house. His children and his wife slept inside, and there were mornings when they had recounted their dreams, or sounds they thought they heard. But he was the one who knew the spirit of the house.

He stopped outside on the porch where the fireplace rose up from a footing poured from concrete and river stone. His hands traveled over the surface, not to read as if by Braille, but to get the house on his skin. Under his palm the rock was still warm from the sun. When he closed his eyes he imagined that the rock was really the face of someone very old and that there was a very old story coming from the lips.

It was a story of the river, the old river. And this old man was telling his river story of the night he had walked down to the bank just as the man from Saginaw had done and just as he would do soon. He removed his clothes and waded into chest-deep water, then lay down on his back. Instead of moving downstream he felt himself held up by strong, soft hands. He never rolled toward her, or made a move to see her face. But he knew in the oldness of the memory he had been with the river woman. How she had moved through him all night, washing in and out, leaving his head clean, electric.

After he lifted his fingers from the rock he stood very still on the porch, then went inside to sleep. On the wall, across from the foot of his bed, he looked into an old print from Saginaw. There was a brook trout rising out of the water, a film of silver light hanging around its body. He closed his eyes and waited for the fish to come in the dream, but instead dreamed of old river stones. How they waited somewhere on the bottom in the bend below the house for a new man to come down, lift them up into a wall of stone where he might come in the night to listen to whispers, to feel a touch of the river woman's lips.

In the dream he stood again on the porch, felt the rock turn to skin, how the flesh moved like water. She bent close to his ear, set the dream deep in his head, each word moving into him like a hook.

The Wager

There was an older man and a younger one, then. Both of them given over to the ritual of opening day. They exchanged small gifts—a box of flies for the older one, a new line for the younger. Then, as they had done every opening day for the last twenty years they walked to the window and stared out into the woods. There was an early morning mist. It was that last Saturday in April when both men sensed in each other that pull in the imagination, replaying each pool and run a hundredfold in the brief time they looked toward the river.

Now the low morning sun was shining in the windows, glinting off the dishes on the table. There were two places. The older one would sit at the end farthest from the kitchen while the younger one would sit at the opposite end of the table. They sat down and exchanged a few words at first, being careful, as men often are, not to break the religion of the moment. Were this a painting, both would appear pensive, tentative, as if the moment might somehow escape and there would be no fishing, no summers or seasons together on the river. They drank their wine slowly. A plum wine always reserved for this one morning in spring. There would be pancakes, and hard-cooked bacon, crisp and dry, the way they both liked it.

It was not a day for stories, and each man had grown accustomed to the silence of the other. They rose from the table and cleared the dishes into the sink. It was then the younger one noticed the two small glasses on the back of the counter filled with clear water and a layer of tiny insects on the bottom. The older one explained that he had found them in the stomachs of two browns he had caught earlier in the morning. "Nymphs," he said, "probably Hendrickson's." And the younger one drew closer, lifted the glass in the light and looked at the perfection of their tiny legs, their minute wing cases bulging slightly.

Then, there came what they now refer to as "the wager," which linked them forever into a fraternity of two. The older one took the glass from the younger, raised it to his mouth, and took a long, slow drink, first the water, then entire bottom contents. "Nymphs," he said, "are good luck," placing the empty glass lightly on the counter.

Before the younger one could speak, the older one set the challenge. "We fish for two hours, streamers, on the short section from Pine Road to the flats. Once back, if your catch is smallest, you drink the second glass. If I lose, the Garrison is yours."

For a long moment the word *Garrison* stuck in his head. *Garrison*, and already he began to build images of the finest rod he had ever seen resting in his hand, casting even more exquisitely than the older one had taught.

Outside, on the porch, they gathered up their gear, talked the small talk of fishermen about to enter holy experience, then stood for a moment face to face, to shake hands, offer good luck. At the end of the ritual, the younger one looked straight into the older one. "You're on," he mumbled, and headed out.

Once at the river, the older one took the lead as he always did. Each cast took him into the tightest pockets, the best runs. He laid out line in slow motion, and the younger one watched for several minutes before he let him get out of sight around the first bend.

For a long time the younger one strained and worked on his rod. He "put" the line places instead of letting it find its place, as the older one had shown. For an hour he fished in what he thought were good pockets, the streamer dancing in the dark water.

Several times he felt the mouths of fish but came up with nothing.

Once around the bend he looked downriver for the older one. Nothing. No trace, as if the fog had taken him in. Then, on a cedar sweeper he found a small, scrawled note: "20 inches. See you at the house in an hour."

Instantly, the younger one grew more boylike. He swallowed hard, imagining walking into the house without a fish, his throat already working against itself, preparing for the contents of the second glass. For a moment he felt himself almost crying, then he began to fish again, almost with a vengeance. He was working the streamer into impossible places, all the while imagining the older one holding the twenty-inch fish in his hands.

For the next half hour he attacked the spots the older one had shown him. The streamer was beginning to move more rhythmically. Then, half in dream, his eyes heavy from rising before the alarm went off at five, he felt the strike. Automatically, he raised the rod tip, letting the fish work back against the reel. All sign of the second glass had vanished. He was winning.

He reeled slowly, then lifted the fat brown into his net, unhooked it, and laid it down.

In the short brown grass on the bank he flattened the fish out, then took out his tape. Carefully, he surveyed its length, counting to himself, "sixteen . . . seventeen . . . eighteen . . . eighteen and a half . . . eighteen and three-quarters . . . damn . . . damn!" and he caught himself. It was over. He knew it. If he didn't lose because of his fish, he would lose on the clock. Quickly he laid the fish in his creel, stood up, and bolted off through the woods.

When he walked in the door, the older one was standing at the sink, his back toward him. "Well, I guess you lost," he said, and turned, grinning at the younger one.

93

"Here's one, at least, eighteen and three-quarters, but it's not over twenty. Gimme the glass."

The older one stopped his hand. "Just a minute," he said "Take a look."

For a second the younger one stared into the sink. He counted to himself: one . . . two. And there in the basin lay two perfectly speckled ten-inch brook trout.

"Twenty inches," the older one said under his breath.

"But . . . but," the younger stammered, reaching for the glass, his face contorted into disgust and loss.

"No, it's not really fair. A trick isn't a win. Here, take the rod."

The younger one held out his hand and felt the bamboo come to life. For five minutes he said nothing, moving his hands up and down the length of the cane, turning it, then reading the older one's name inscribed on the butt plate.

"Now it's yours," the older said. "You earned it."

He held the rod for a long time, half smiling, almost weeping. Then, in a rush of movement, almost as if swirling toward something both seen and unseen, almost as if striking the glass, the younger raised it to his lips, drank in the water first, then the nymphs, slapping it down in front of the older one as he finished.

Titles in the Great Lakes Books Series

Freshwater Fury: Yarns and Reminiscences of the Greatest Storm in Inland Navigation, by Frank Barcus, 1986 (reprint)

Call It North Country: The Story of Upper Michigan, by John Bartlow Martin, 1986 (reprint)

The Land of the Crooked Tree, by U. P. Hedrick, 1986 (reprint)

Michigan Place Names, by Walter Romig, 1986 (reprint)

Luke Karamazov, by Conrad Hilberry, 1987

The Late, Great Lakes: An Environmental History, by William Ashworth, 1987 (reprint)

Great Pages of Michigan History from the Detroit Free Press, 1987

Waiting for the Morning Train: An American Boyhood, by Bruce Catton, 1987 (reprint)

Michigan Voices: Our State's History in the Words of the People Who Lived it, compiled and edited by Joe Grimm, 1987

Danny and the Boys, Being Some Legends of Hungry Hollow, by Robert Traver, 1987 (reprint)

Hanging On, or How to Get through a Depression and Enjoy Life, by Edmund G. Love, 1987 (reprint)

The Situation in Flushing, by Edmund G. Love, 1987 (reprint)

A Small Bequest, by Edmund G. Love, 1987 (reprint)

The Saginaw Paul Bunyan, by James Stevens, 1987 (reprint)

The Ambassador Bridge: A Monument to Progress, by Philip P. Mason, 1988

Let the Drum Beat: A History of the Detroit Light Guard, by Stanley D. Solvick, 1988

An Afternoon in Waterloo Park, by Gerald Dumas, 1988 (reprint)

Contemporary Michigan Poetry: Poems from the Third Coast, edited by Michael Delp, Conrad Hilberry, and Herbert Scott, 1988

Over the Graves of Horses, by Michael Delp, 1988

Wolf in Sheep's Clothing: The Search for a Child Killer, by Tommy McIntyre, 1988

Copper-Toed Boots, by Marguerite de Angeli, 1989 (reprint)

Detroit Images: Photographs of the Renaissance City, edited by John J. Bukowczyk and Douglas Aikenhead, with Peter Slavcheff, 1989

Hangdog Reef: Poems Sailing the Great Lakes, by Stephen Tudor, 1989

Detroit: City of Race and Class Violence, revised edition, by B. J. Widick, 1989

Deep Woods Frontier: A History of Logging in Northern Michigan, by Theodore J. Karamanski, 1989

Orvie, The Dictator of Dearborn, by David L. Good, 1989

Seasons of Grace: A History of the Catholic Archdiocese of Detroit, by Leslie Woodcock Tentler, 1990

The Pottery of John Foster: Form and Meaning, by Gordon and Elizabeth Orear, 1990